Original title:
Tassels in the Breeze

Author: Natalia Harrington
ISBN HARDBACK: 978-1-80586-126-3
ISBN PAPERBACK: 978-1-80586-598-8

Colors Adrift in Air

Little flags wave, bright and clear,
Caught in a dance, free of fear.
Spinning like tops, what a sight,
They giggle and twirl in pure delight.

A splash of red, a hint of blue,
They seem to say, 'We're here for you!'
In the wind's gentle hold, they sway,
Laughing with joy come what may.

Fluttering Memories of Fabric

Oh, those scraps from years gone by,
Whirling around, oh my, oh my!
Each thread recalls a secret cheer,
Silly moments, woven near.

Grandma’s quilt with stories told,
In the wind, it dances bold.
With every flap, nostalgia calls,
Sewing memories in fragile squalls.

Breezy Serenade of Threads

Strings take flight in the sunny air,
Bouncing along without a care.
A whimsical tune begins to play,
As lively gusts invite the fray.

Whispering secrets, they twist and turn,
Like playful kittens, eager to learn.
With every flip, a giggle bursts,
In this fabric ballet, joy is immersed.

Wands of Airy Textures

Wands of color dart and weave,
Teasing the breeze, they dance and cleave.
In a flutter, they make you grin,
Lighthearted laughter, let’s begin!

Textures playful, soft and bright,
Caressing the air with pure delight.
As if to say, 'Join the fun!'
Under the sky, we are all one.

Threads of Whimsy

In a world where yarns take flight,
The playful threads seek out the light.
With a wink and a twirl, they tease the air,
Dancing with glee, shedding each care.

A stitch here and there, a giggle's sound,
Spinning a tale that whirls around.
Each loop is a laugh, each knot a cheer,
They frolic and prance, spreading good cheer.

Dancing Fragments in the Wind

Little bits of chaos swirl and sway,
In sunny skies or cloudy gray.
They whirl in circles, they tumble and play,
Bright bits of laughter, they brighten the day.

With a flick of a wrist, they dash and dart,
These quirky fragments have a certain art.
A fabric joke that lifts the gloom,
Tickling the breeze as they twirl and zoom.

Whispers of Color and Air

Colors giggle in the afternoon glow,
Whispering secrets as they ebb and flow.
Playful hues skip through the skies,
Crafting a tale that never dies.

With each soft brush, they tease and taunt,
Hues of delight in a joyful flaunt.
Twisting and turning, their laughter's a thrill,
Painting the world with a whimsical will.

Fluttering Echoes of Fabric

Echoes of fabric rustle and sing,
With every flutter, they bring a zing.
They tease the passerby with glee,
Flapping their joy, wild and free.

In every dip and rise, there’s laughter anew,
As they tumble through time, just like morning dew.
Sewn with a smile, they tickle the breeze,
Chasing the sun, with whimsical ease.

Windswept Whispers of the Past

When the wind gave a chuckle,
Old hats danced with delight.
Memories twirled and jiggled,
As kites took off in flight.

Nostalgic tales took wing,
Glad socks found their lost mates.
With each gust, laughter rang,
As past joys shifted states.

Harmonies Woven into the Air

The breeze strummed on my ribs,
Like strings of a grand guitar.
Socks flailed in cheeky flips,
As if they'd just come from afar.

Whistles of glee came around,
Chasing the clouds in delight.
Even the old trees spun round,
As if they were dancing all night.

Cerulean Hues on a Gentle Zephyr

Soft whispers painted blue,
With splashes of laughter too.
Hats flipped like pancakes high,
In a game known but to few.

Sunshine peeked through the fluff,
As if dressed in silly guise.
Each gust brought forth the stuff,
Of giggles and surprised eyes.

Breezy Notes from a Loomed Tale

A melody puffed and played,
On the streamers and the flags.
Caught in a whimsical trade,
As even the sparrows wag.

The air held jokes at the seams,
Tickling the leaves so bright.
A tapestry built of dreams,
Danced to the winds' delight.

Medley of Sun-kissed Streamers

Fluttering bright, they twirl and sway,
Like little party hats on a sunny day.
Chasing the wind, they burst with glee,
A jolly parade, just wait and see.

With giggles and wiggles, they flip and flop,
A carnival joy that just won't stop.
They tease the air with a playful grin,
Inviting all to join in their spin.

Fringing Dances in the Light

In the bright glow, they dart and dive,
Jiving and jiggling, oh, they come alive!
A colorful crew with no fear of heights,
Waving their arms in wild delight.

They shimmy and shake as shadows befriend,
Light-hearted laughter that seems to transcend.
Like silly confetti on a joyous spree,
Unruly dancers, come twirl with me!

Whirling Among the Shadows

Spinning like tops in a shadowed play,
They don’t mind the night, prefer it that way.
Whispers of jest in the cool evening air,
A frolicsome band, without any care.

They prance through the dark, making shapes on the ground,
Like floppety fish that jiggle around.
Giggling shadows in a merry-go-loop,
A quirky carnival of an invisible troupe.

Unraveled Stitches of Time

Threads of laughter, unspooling bright,
Sewing together both day and night.
Snapping like rubber bands tossed in delight,
Each moment is stitched with sheer instinct.

Tangled impressions that tickle the mind,
Loose ends hanging, hilariously unrefined.
With every twist and turn along the way,
The fabric of fun we stitch and replay.

Whims of Wayward Strands

Upon a whim, the threads take flight,
Chasing birds in morning light.
They trip and tumble, laugh and spin,
A knotted mess, they pull you in.

A dance of colors, bright and bold,
They whisper secrets, stories told.
Each twist and turn, a playful tease,
A tangled tale swayed by the breeze.

Castles in the Air of Fabric

In dreams, we weave with threads so grand,
Constructing castles on soft land.
But lo! They flutter, take a dive,
Become a blanket, oh what a jive!

The towers lean, the flags they flop,
Each stitch a giggle, cannot stop.
A whimsy home, where nothing's right,
Who needs a plan? Let's take to flight!

Symphony of Sunlit Fringes

Under the sun, fringes play tunes,
A symphony sung by colorful boons.
They twirl and jig, oh what a sight,
Like a parade in sheer delight.

The harmonies dance, a wavy cheer,
With each soft sway, we’ve naught to fear.
Oh, what a concert, fabrics unite,
Turning our worries into sheer light.

The Dance of Colorful Winds

The playful wind, a jester bold,
Takes vibrant strands and gives them hold.
They prance and play, oh what a prize,
Transforming smiles, the world's surprise.

They leap and swirl in joyful spin,
A total riot; let the fun begin!
Each flick a giggle, a breezy cheer,
Join the chaotic dance, oh dear!

The Art of Floating Memories

A hat on the line, swinging in glee,
Recalling lost love, or maybe just tea.
Chasing the sun with a playful shout,
As shadows of laughter begin to sprout.

Birds giggle and snicker, plucking the thread,
They dance with the wind, fill skies overhead.
A kite full of secrets, drifting so free,
Reminds me of socks lost at the laundry spree.

Celestial Fabrications in the Air.

Bananas on branches, the squirrels do stare,
While clouds knit a blanket, with whimsical flair.
Stars wink in the night, like a cheeky surprise,
While moonbeams play tag, under open skies.

The sun paints the dawn, with splashes of gold,
As giggling blossoms in gardens unfold.
A butterfly teases, with colors so bright,
In a world intertwined, it sways left and right.

Whispers of Frayed Threads

Elastic adventures on whimsical routes,
Where tumbleweeds tango, resembling hoots.
Snippets of laughter, in wind's wild embrace,
Unraveling stories, in a light-hearted race.

A patchwork of joy, sewn with comic strands,
Made by the mischief of playful hands.
Each whisper and giggle, a knot in the air,
Floating like daisies without any care.

Dance of the Fluttering Fringes

A flutter of fabric, with a cheeky grin,
Sprinkling joy like confetti in the din.
Napping on porches, in a breezy retreat,
Where giggles and snorts blend, oh what a feat!

They twist in the sunlight, joyful and loose,
A parade of mishaps, in chaos, profuse.
Life’s silly dance is a romp without end,
Through twirling and swirling, we all just pretend.

Threads that Flutter and Dream

In a garden full of kite strings,
Laughter dances on the wind,
A sock hops with a giggle,
While trousers twirl, no end.

Underneath the sunny sky,
A scarf does the cha-cha slide,
The hats all take their chances,
In this light-hearted glide.

Breezy whims and silly caps,
Jumpsuits have a comic flair,
With every flip and every twist,
Fashion finds itself laid bare.

Threads that come alive to play,
Tickling toes with every sway,
So join this merry, rustling crowd,
And laugh out loud, oh laugh out loud!

The Dust of Wandering Veils

A feather boa flaps and flirts,
With every gust, it gives a spin,
While veils of tulle, like ghosts, have fun,
Doing twirls and chiming grins.

A curtain sneaks a peek, oh dear,
Not wanting to be left behind,
Catching on a gust, it swirls,
As if rehearsing for a kind.

Ribbons twist like slinky charms,
They find each other, dance and play,
Who knew that fabrics had such dreams,
And could surprise us in such way?

Dust bunnies cheer for their own show,
In corners where the breezes blow,
Each swing and laugh in perfect time,
Making this funny life a rhyme!

Garden of Floating Textiles

In a patch of cozy colors bright,
Bloomed a garden where clothes take flight,
A pair of shorts tried to impress,
With a wiggly dance of pure finesse.

The shirts are giggling, twirling wide,
As pants play hide and seek with pride,
Remember that old woolly hat?
It leaps and bounds—imagine that!

The sundresses laugh in floral hues,
Deciding which breeze to choose,
With every flutter, laughter grows,
Sprinkling joy in fabric flows.

Under the sun, they play all day,
Wearing smiles that float away,
In this whimsical, woven space,
Every stitch wears a grin of grace!

Fluttering Touch of the Day

As morning breaks with breezy cheer,
With playful ribbons dancing near,
A handkerchief pops up to say,
'Let’s frolic in this light today!'

The bow ties bounce, no worries found,
In tussled grass, they leap around,
While capes provide a superhero flair,
Spreading joy throughout the air.

Bright socks find barrels of delight,
Climbing fences for a better height,
While jackets hug and giggle tease,
In the breeze that never flees.

A playful air, a funny blend,
Of textiles twirling, curves to bend,
Join this laughter filled display,
Where colors join the dance of play!

Parading Fancies under the Sun

Bright colors flutter high,
Like squirrels on a spree.
Dancing shadows pass us by,
What a sight to see!

Gaily strutting down the lane,
A parade of silly hats.
Each one sporting such a gain,
With feathers and with splats!

Funny hops and little twirls,
As laughter lights the air.
The sun reflects on playful whirls,
No spot was left unfair!

Now we all join in the fun,
With giggles all around.
A fanciful and sunny run,
Where joy can always be found!

Fragments of Joy Ambling Along

A skipping stone with goofy grace,
It leaps and hops so free.
A neighbor's cat, in such a chase,
Is quite the sight to see!

Bicycles with squeaky wheels,
Racing past the park.
Each twist and turn spins such appeals,
Adventures never dark.

Sidewalk art of chalky dreams,
With colors, big, and bold.
Giggles burst like sunshine beams,
As stories now unfold.

So let's just stroll and laugh aloud,
With smiles that brighten gray.
Each moment shared brings joy unbowed,
In silly, fun display!

A Tapestry’s Breath on a Whisper

Wind carries secrets soft and bright,
Whirling through the trees.
A curious tune in morning light,
Plays tricks like bumblebees.

Waving leaves join in the song,
Their laughter fills the space.
Nature's grace is never wrong,
Always wearing a smiley face!

With grassy patches here and there,
A duel of ants ensues.
Who’ll win this tiny sport affair?
With no time for the blues!

Time to bask in this delight,
Embrace the quirky scene.
With giggles shared, hearts feel so light,
In nature's silly glean.

Sun-kissed Skirts of Nature

The flowers twirl in vibrant skirts,
Like dancers in the clay.
They giggle softly, toss their spirts,
In a bright, carefree way.

Bees buzzing like a silly band,
Each one with a funny tune.
While butterflies in grand demand,
Are flirting with the moon.

The trees join in with rustling leaves,
A chorus full of laughs.
Like playful children on the eves,
They share their tales in drafts.

So let's embrace this silly spree,
In nature's grand parade.
With sunshine bright and hearts so free,
Let fun never evade!

Shimmering Particles Amongst Leaves

Dancing dust in sunlight's glow,
Giggles of leaves, soft and low.
A flutter here, a twist of fate,
Nature’s confetti, oh so great!

Silly shadows skipping fast,
Whispering secrets from the past.
A swirl of fun, a merry chase,
As laughter fills each hidden space.

Lyrical Streams of Material

Whimsical winds tease the cloth,
Turning tails like curious sloths.
A merry jig, a playful knot,
Who knew ribbons liked to trot?

Bouncing bright in summer's light,
Fabric frolics, what a sight!
With every twist, a giggle spun,
Dresses dancing, oh how fun!

Vibrant Whirls Beneath the Sky

Swirling colors, bold and free,
Fleeting friends, just like me.
Around we go, in joyful twirl,
As chaos reigns and ribbons whirl!

Cotton candy clouds in play,
Chasing dreams, we lose our way.
In this laughter, we all trust,
To find the magic in the dust.

Frayed Edges with a Story

Old threads laughing, worn and wise,
Tales of travels, sweet surprise.
Each little snag, a hint of cheer,
In every fray, a story near.

Grandma’s quilt is quite the muse,
With every patch, it sings the blues.
Stitched with joy and laughter's grace,
Life’s silly threads in every space.

Swaying Anthems of the Afternoon

In the park, a hat does fly,
Chasing pigeons, oh my, oh my!
Straw on heads, a jaunty style,
Catching glances, making smiles.

Giggling children dash about,
With ice cream cones, they twist and shout.
A gentle breeze, the laughter swells,
As squirrels plan their nutty spells.

Picnic blankets spread with glee,
Surprising ants, oh can't you see?
Burgers flip, some peppers dance,
Food thus flung, a tasty chance.

Each silly hat upon the grass,
A fashion show, alas, alas!
With ribbons trailing, oh what grace,
The afternoon, a funny place.

Colorful Ribbons off the Rails

On the train, with stops galore,
Kids waving flags, oh what a score!
Bright colors fly with joyful cheer,
As engineers just scratch their beard.

A lady's scarf, it waves so free,
A gust, and now it's up a tree!
Conductors laugh, a funny sight,
As ribbons race with all their might.

An old man snores with such a grin,
His hat takes flight, it starts to spin.
As passengers all crack a smile,
The kind of joy that lasts a while.

Through tunnels dark, with laughter bright,
The train of dreams departs the night.
With every jolt and colorful flare,
Life's little moments fill the air.

The Gentle Dance of a Summer’s Day

Sunshine filters through the trees,
Dancers twirl with the light breeze.
Grasshoppers jump, a lively croon,
While bees buzz tunes, under the moon.

A toddler slips and starts to giggle,
Chasing shadows, oh what a wiggle!
Flip-flops fly as runners race,
With laughter bright, they set the pace.

A family picnic, who forgot the pie?
A seagull swoops, oh my, oh my!
With a beak so bold, it steals a fry,
While doggies bark, we can't deny.

The day's a whirl, with smiles and play,
Every moment seems to sway.
Through giggles, snacks, and blushing cheeks,
Summer’s dance is all it seeks.

Stitched Memories on the Wind

A quilt unfolds upon the lawn,
With stories stitched, from dusk till dawn.
Grandma’s tale of cats so spry,
Is met with gasps and joyful sighs.

The wind plays tricks, it lifts a fork,
Sent flying past a startled stork!
As sandwiches take flight, oh dear,
The butterflies just laugh and cheer.

With lemonade that fizzes high,
And crumbs that fly, oh my, oh my!
The ants parade with crumbly pride,
As kids all run, the fun won't hide.

Each little stitch, a laugh, a sound,
Is woven tight in joy profound.
On the breeze, our stories send,
Making memories that never end.

Liquid Hues on Soft Breezes

Colors dance in the air,
Like silly fish in a stream.
They shimmer and sway with flair,
Tickling our minds like a dream.

Swirling shades, a comic sight,
Chasing butterflies on a spree.
A rainbow wiggles with delight,
All while sipping iced tea.

Giggling leaves in playful cheer,
Bouncing as if they're alive.
Whispering secrets, oh so near,
In the sun, they gleefully thrive.

Oh, the sunlight joins the show,
Gliding softly on the breeze.
With every laugh and every glow,
Nature's pageant helps us tease.

Poetic Kites in the Sun

Kites soar high, like playful glee,
Chasing clouds with joyous spins.
They perform in the light so free,
A symphony of colorful wins.

Twisting tails—a ballet scene,
Dancing wildly in the blue.
As they delve and twirl, they preen,
With silly leaps, they break through.

Each loop a giggle, a flair,
As they tangle in the air.
Caught in breezes, unaware,
They flirt with skies, a funny pair.

And when they dip, oh, what a sight!
Racing down in a flurry.
It's pure joy, what a delight,
In the sun, they dance in the hurry.

The Almost-Whispers of Patterns

Patterns play in snippets small,
They giggle, twirl, and sway at will.
In every corner, they enthrall,
With swirls that give our brains a thrill.

Like kittens chasing fuzzy dreams,
Squirming and wriggling on the ground.
They whisper secrets in sunbeams,
In tangled threads, they're laughter bound.

Wobbly lines and polka dots,
They prance and bounce into a spree.
Oh, what nonsense patterns plot,
In this cheerful lunacy!

So let them sway, those funny shapes,
In a world where colors clash.
We giggle at their silly scrapes,
While chaos layers each wild dash.

Shimmering Echoes of Airborne Threads

Threads of laughter in the skies,
Watch them waddle, jig, and prance.
Just like birds with funny ties,
They spin and twirl in a dance.

Each shimmering wisp takes a chance,
To trip over the clouds so round.
With every twist and every glance,
They scatter giggles on the ground.

Floating high, weaving in pairs,
Like joyful whispers on a spree.
Tickling noses, ruffling hairs,
Embracing all with glee and glee.

What a sight, this airborne spree,
Where threads frolic in the sun.
Here's to joy, forever free,
In this laughter-laden run.

The Hex of Windy Tendrils

A knot of strings in a dance so rare,
They twist and twirl in the daytime air.
A gusty chuckle from a playful breeze,
Makes a wiggly sight that's sure to please.

They loop and flutter, a merry parade,
A jester's hat in a frolicsome spade.
Swaying with mischief, they bounce around,
Entwined in laughter, no sorrow found.

With every zigzag, a giggling flair,
No proper fashion, just flair everywhere!
Windy enchantments weave tales so sly,
To tickle your heart and make spirits fly.

But hold on tight, here comes a big blow!
A jinx of whirlwinds, stealing the show.
Ah, there they go with a silly cheer;
A merry mishap—oh dear, oh dear!

Captured Melodies in Motion

Dancing ribbons play a symphony bright,
As they waltz through the streets in delight.
With each little swirl, they giggle and sway,
Singing sweet tunes that float far away.

They flutter high, then dive down low,
Doing a jig as they steal the show.
A perplexed pigeon gives them a stare,
While a dog interrupts with a joyful flare.

Oh listen closely, the giggles are near,
A chorus of mischief that's sure to cheer.
These carefree notes in the air take flight,
Bringing laughter to dawn and sweetening night.

Each twist and turn, they flit with glee,
A melody caught, oh how funny to see!
They dance in the sunlight, a fresh serenade,
While the world joins the fun, in this grand parade.

Ebb and Flow of Nature's Stitches

In patterns of chaos, a yarn takes its form,
As giggling strands weather each storm.
A patchwork of color, wild as your thought,
With every twist, a new humor is caught.

They bob and weave like a playful thread,
A ticklish tapestry, laughter widespread.
Caught in the moments, they swing and swoosh,
Tickling the sky in a soft, breezy push.

Oh, watch them loop like a comical quilt,
Stitched with laughter, no sign of guilt.
Bit by bit, they tease the light,
Playful fibers making fun of the night.

Each ebb and flow brings a smile to the face,
As nature conspires in this colorful race.
With knots of hilarity, together they soar,
A patch of mirth by the wide-open door.

Streamers of Skyward Whispers

In a circus of colors, the whispers arise,
Chatty streamers crowd the vast, open skies.
Breezy giggles ride on the currents of fun,
In a wacky ballet beneath the bright sun.

They swoop and glide in a ticklish loop,
Making clouds chuckle, oh what a troop!
Down they tumble, like mischievous sprites,
Creating a ruckus in sweet soaring flights.

With every flutter, a secret's unveiled,
A joke from the wind, oh how it prevailed.
A parade of whispers, hilarious chatter,
Each teasing breeze brings forth playful matter.

So join in the laughter, let spirits run free,
With ribbons of mirth dancing wild as can be.
For skyward secrets and jolly displays,
Bring forth the giggles in whimsical ways.

Along the Edge of the Wind

A squirrel in a tutu twirls,
Chasing gusts with tiny curls.
Laughter spills from every tree,
As leaves giggle, wild and free.

A kite caught high in a swirl,
Does flips and tricks with a whirl.
The sun grins wide, no frown in sight,
While balloons float off in delight.

A dog leaps up, thinks he can fly,
Chasing shadows flitting by.
Oh, the chaos in this breeze,
Nature’s jest, just meant to tease.

But a hat escapes my crown,
Somersaulting, upside down.
It lands on a laughing llama's head,
And off they trot, the wind ahead.

Swaying Hues of Sunlit Dreams

A grasshopper in polka dots,
Jumps on clouds, connecting knots.
Each leap a giggle, such delight,
As butterflies dance, oh what a sight!

The sun spills paint on the street,
As colors blend in rhythmic beat.
Balloons wobble, chasing the light,
Their squeaks and pops bring sheer delight.

An old cat snoozes on a fence,
Dreaming of tuna with no pretense.
While a cheerful breeze tugs his tail,
He wakes to laughter on the trail.

Each vine and flower sways and swerves,
In this comical dance, it preserves.
Moments of joy, perfectly bright,
As everyone joins in the flight.

Embers of a Gentle Gale

A bearded dragon on a kite,
Sails through clouds, oh what a sight!
With each gust, he waves and grins,
As laughter bubbles, joy begins.

A picnic blanket flies away,
Chasing ants who've come to play.
Sandwiches caught in the swirl,
Flying off with a jump and twirl.

Juggling lemons, a clown appears,
With fruity mirth, he cheers and cheers.
But who can catch a squirming snack?
A swift wind aids his comic act.

The fireflies giggle, blink, and glow,
Dancing with pride, stealing the show.
Embers flicker beneath the trees,
As all join in the evening's tease.

Ribbons of Twilight Air

A raccoon dons a sailor's hat,
Steering pies through the world of chat.
While moonlight winks with playful tunes,
And stars tap dance, making swoons.

A hedgehog with a tiny flag,
Marches in style, oh what a brag!
The night bumps with a silly beat,
As owls join in, an echoing tweet.

A firefly plays peek-a-boo,
Lighting up the tales, meant for two.
Each flicker sparks a giggling spree,
As shadows dance, wild and free.

In this twilight, laughter flies,
With every swirl, the fun multiplies.
Ribbons of joy float through the air,
In this night of whimsy, without a care.

Sun-kissed Bowls of Joy

In the garden, laughter flocks,
Bright colors dance on sunny clocks.
Whimsical hats with feathers sway,
Joyful antics on display.

Chasing shadows, we do twirl,
Bouncing like oversized pearls.
Fruit flies join the jolly show,
Nature's laughter in tow.

Bouncing balls and silly sounds,
Mirthful chaos all around.
Sipped lemonade and cheeky smiles,
Playfulness extends for miles.

Under the sun, joy does spill,
Tickling toes, a leaping thrill.
In this bowl, we find delight,
Sun-kissed days and sheer delight.

Currents of Ethereal Strands

Winds play tricks with curls and hats,
Stirring strands like playful cats.
Balloons bounce in the air's embrace,
Cheeky wind wants to race.

Waving flags of fabric cheer,
Dancing whims that disappear.
A kite flys just out of reach,
It teases, time for a speech!

Strands of laughter on the line,
Merry whispers, oh so fine.
In the wind, we toss our schemes,
Crafting laughter from our dreams.

Oh, the fun of tangled plight,
Ethereal laughs in flight!
Kite runners in a grand parade,
Mirthful chaos, unafraid.

Floating Poetry in the Wind

A paper plane soon takes its chance,
It flutters past, a funny dance.
Words set free from inked up binds,
In jolly whirls, they're hard to find.

Scrolls of laughter on the breeze,
Crafted jokes like dancing leaves.
Pictures drawn with giggles fair,
Twisted tales hang in the air.

Punny verses float on trails,
Whimsical whims, like tiny sails.
Each draft carries a sparkling jest,
Wind's soft chuckle, nature's best.

As giggling whispers intertwine,
Serene chaos feels divine.
Poetry sails, giggles cling,
In the wind, we laugh and sing.

Whirling Embroidery of Dreams

Stitches buzz in silly loops,
Weaving laughter into groups.
Quirky threads of fun and play,
Join the fabric of our day.

Buttons spin with joyful zest,
Silly patterns, surely blessed.
Each yarn dance and playful whirl,
Dreams like ribbons start to twirl.

Frayed edges tell a wacky tale,
As crafty breezes set the sail.
In the thread, our giggles lock,
Whimsical art, off the clock.

Come join in this fabric spree,
With threads of joy, we're wild and free!
Embroidery floats on a whim,
In this dance of dreams, we swim.

The Sorcery of Fabric Flight

Threaded wonders dance with glee,
In a world of whimsy, wild and free.
They flutter, twirl, and take their leave,
A magic show, you won't believe!

With every gust, they laugh and leap,
Playing tricks as secrets keep.
Like cheeky sprites with mischief planned,
They tease the winds across the land.

A swirl of colors, bright and bold,
Their stories in the air retold.
They sing a tune of joyful jive,
In fabric's dance, we feel alive!

So let them spin, with voices proud,
An army of fabric, fierce and loud.
With every flap, they charm and boast,
A feathery sight we love the most.

Airborne Shimmers of Forgotten Times

Once they hung like mundane dreams,
Now they soar on sunlit beams.
Whispers live in swaying hues,
An echo from the past in view.

They giggle softly as they sway,
Reminding us of yesterday.
With every toss, a tale retold,
And memories of laughter bold.

With cheeky grins, they flit around,
Making mischief, sweet and sound.
Old secrets dance, they pop and puff,
Like happy souls who've called their bluff.

Oh, let them whirl with joyous cheer,
A fabric circus drawing near.
In swirling nights or sunny days,
They bring to life a cheerful craze.

Rustling Strands of Laughter

Strands of joy that rustle near,
Bring blushing cheeks and hearts sincere.
They play a tune, a slapstick show,
With giggles floating to and fro.

In every flap, a chuckle swells,
As if they're weaving funny spells.
They twist and turn in silly prance,
Inviting everyone to dance.

A prankster’s game, they love to tease,
Twirling fast in the playful breeze.
Like ribbons full of spirit bright,
They launch into the joyful night.

So come and join this merry flight,
As laughter soars to wondrous height.
With every rustle, every cheer,
The strands of fun are always near!

Gossamer Dreams in the Open

Delicate wisps that float and glide,
They come alive when winds abide.
With glimmers soft, they tease and play,
Creating smiles in light's warm ray.

Invisible threads in bright array,
Whispers of joy in a sunny bay.
They dance around, both sly and spry,
A spectacle we can't deny.

With every kick, a spirit shines,
In fluttering cloaks of rainbow lines.
They beckon forth with gentle sway,
A lighthearted jest that won't decay.

Oh, frolic free, and lose your cares,
In fabric dreams, no need for snares.
For every shimmer, every scroll,
Holds laughter's magic at its soul.

Colorful Notes in the Wind

A sock got loose and danced away,
It twirled and spun, so full of play.
The cat just stared, eyes wide and round,
As socks and leaves both hit the ground.

A handkerchief joined the sock's spree,
It flapped its wings, felt wild and free.
A gust of fun, they laughed and played,
Who knew that laundry had this waylaid?

A ribbon joined in with a cheer,
Floating high, shedding all its fear.
It's funny how a breeze can make,
A party from a laundry mistake!

With colorful notes, they swirled and spun,
Pretending to dance, oh, what fun!
Two mismatched items, what a scene,
In the wild wind, they ruled as queens!

Serenade of Fairytale Flutters

Once upon a time, a hat took flight,
It whirled and twirled with all its might.
A bird in a bow tie joined the fun,
Singing loud 'til the day was done.

A spoon joined in, oh what a sight,
With a fork and a knife, it took to the height.
They pirouetted through the soft cleft,
Chasing a breeze, oh where it left!

A dishcloth waved from the tabletop,
With a gasp of glee, it couldn't stop.
Fairytale dreams in every flap,
Creating laughter in a whimsical lap.

The clock chimed in from its hanging place,
Tick-tock joined in this funny chase.
Tales of joy flew through the air,
And left behind a crazy flair!

Whimsical Weavings of the Day

A pair of mittens tried a new thing,
They tied their strings for joy to bring.
They swayed and jived to a cheerful beat,
Spinning circles, oh what a treat!

With a fabric flower, they formed a crew,
Flipping and flapping as high they grew.
A handkerchief giggled, lost in the fun,
Joined as they leapt, oh how they run!

A stitching group, in colors so bright,
Together they danced as day turned to night.
Mittens and flowers, a sight to behold,
Crafting a story that's never been told.

Through pathways of laughter, they zipped away,
Creating a weaving in the sunny ray.
Such whimsy arose, as they played and twirled,
In this tapestry, joy was unfurled!

Drifting Patterns in the Sun

A checkered napkin spun round and round,
It snickered loudly, quite unbound.
Balloons floated, color and cheer,
In a lively dance, they drew us near.

A jelly bean bounced with delight,
In a wobbly line, it took off in flight.
An old pair of boots joined the race,
Shuffling awkwardly, trying to trace.

The sun beamed down on this playful crew,
Patterns emerged of every hue.
With giggles and snorts, they brightened the lane,
Turning a dull day into a game!

Through loops and twists, they swayed in tune,
Under the watch of a smiling moon.
Drifting together with joy in the sun,
What a funny, lively day had begun!

Luminescent Streams of Color

A squiggle here, a dot of cheer,
They twirl and swirl, a sight so queer.
With every gust, they wave hello,
A vibrant dance, a funny show.

They tease the wind with giggles bright,
A rainbow prank in soft daylight.
Silly pirouettes, never shy,
Joking with clouds that float on by.

Flickering shades, a joyful mess,
Each twist and turn, pure happiness.
They mock the trees, a gentle tease,
With colors bold, they dance with ease.

So let them laugh, these hues of glee,
In playful jests, we all agree.
For life's a canvas, wild and fun,
Where laughter's woven, everyone!

The Tails of Forgotten Tales

Once they flew, on adventure's ride,
With swirling stories, side by side.
Yet in the attic, gathering dust,
Their playful paths now lost in rust.

They whisper now in giggles slight,
Of daring dreams that took to flight.
A dragon's tail, a knight's old shoe,
Oh what a tale, if only true!

Each wrinkle holds a wacky plot,
From treasure hunts to silly spots.
They wiggled high and flopped quite low,
Like sock puppets, putting on a show.

But in the breeze, they find a way,
To dance again, bright in their play.
So let's resurrect these threads of yore,
Where laughter echoes, forevermore!

Kites of Ethereal Fabric

They pirouette in the shimmering skies,
Chasing the clouds, oh what a surprise!
With every tug, they giggle and swoop,
A colorful crew in a frolicking loop.

In the breeze, they play tag with the sun,
Whirling and twirling, what silly fun!
With strings like noodles all tangled and knotted,
They bob and weave, never overwhelmed, not once spotted.

A pocket of joy, a wild array,
Floppy and floppy, they frolic and sway.
Each flutter a chuckle, a hearty little jest,
Kites in the air, the very best fest.

So let them dance, these windswept sprites,
Painting the sky in colorful flights.
With laughter that echoes, they take to the blue,
Creating fun, just for me and you!

Ephemeral Dance of Colors

Oh what a sight, colors collide,
They hop and skip with giddy pride.
A fleeting flash, like a comet's tail,
Bouncing about, they giggle and wail.

A polka-dot jig, a striped ballet,
Who knew they'd dance, in this wild way?
Each shade a prankster, bright and bold,
Sharing their antics, never controlled.

They shimmer and sparkle, a giggly spree,
Silly flames of joy, fluttering free.
Each tiny swish, a whimsical play,
Creating a ruckus, come join the fray!

Yet as they flicker, they're bound to flee,
Reminding us life's a grand jubilee.
So laugh with the hues, feel joy that ignites,
In this ephemeral dance, our heart takes flight!

Swaying Ribbons of Memory

In the wind, they dance around,
Like joyful thoughts unbound.
A twist here and a twirl there,
Whisking laughter through the air.

Every flutter tells a tale,
Of a kite that tried to sail.
With mishaps sewn in every seam,
Who knew a ribbon had a dream?

They stick to trees and twist in knots,
Chasing squirrels, stirring plots.
I tried to catch one as it flew,
But it giggled and just flew right through.

So I sat back and watched the show,
Of colors bright and movement flow.
In a world of fluffy delight,
Those ribbons spun my day so bright.

Driftwood and Floating Stitches

On the shore where misfits play,
Driftwood winks at the end of the day.
Floating stitches in a seam,
Weaving tales that make you beam.

A piece of wood tells a grand old joke,
As seagulls squawk and the dolphins poke.
They frolic in their salty show,
While driftwood waves and steals the flow.

Each wave brings a new shiny bit,
While stubborn logs refuse to sit.
They jostle for space, shimmy with glee,
Saying, “Look at me, I'm fancy and free!”

But oh, when the tide starts to roll,
The driftwood knows it’s lost its goal.
It laughs off the sun and drifts away,
In currents bold, it’s the life of the day.

The Sauntering Tides of Color

The tides decide to strut their stuff,
With splashes of shades that are quite enough.
Waves pirouette in a colorful spree,
As jellyfish laugh in their jellyfish glee.

Underneath the sun's bright gaze,
The water sparkles in a wavy haze.
I'm almost convinced the sea knows how,
To throw a party—oh, take a bow!

Fish flip in funky disco moves,
While crabs join in the groovy grooves.
Seaweed's swaying with all its might,
Under the moon, such a hilarious sight.

I took a dip to join the fun,
But tripped on a conch and ruined my run.
Yet laughter's echo fills the salty air,
As I float out, colorful without a care.

Flare of Wind-swept Textures

Textures tumbling, a wild parade,
Each fabric flutters, a charming charade.
From silky slips to rugged twine,
They play peek-a-boo, oh how they shine!

Caught in breezes that jig and laugh,
They dance like kids in a crazy craft.
Ribbons coated in spicy scents,
Swirling up tales where no one laments.

A sock escapes from the laundry line,
While a tablecloth tries to do just fine.
"Catch me if you can!" they slyly tease,
Stirring up giggles, like buzzing bees.

Even the dishes join in the fun,
The spoons start spinning; oh, what a run!
In the flare of textures, wild and free,
A fest of laughter, just let it be!

Chasing the Soft Serenade

In a world where giggles dart,
Swaying gently, a light-hearted art.
Maracas jingle, laughter flows,
We chase the tune where the wild wind blows.

Whirling hats on heads askew,
A dance of clowns, with antics new.
With every spin, we stumble and twirl,
In this silly show, we laugh and whirl.

Feathers flutter from the skies,
As tricks unfold before our eyes.
Banana peels become our stage,
In this comic play, we turn the page.

With playful hearts, we strike a pose,
Joking 'bout the chaos that follows us close.
A soft serenade leads us away,
In the rhythm of fun, we choose to play.

Flickering Banners of Light

Waving colors with a zing,
Silly shadows dance and cling.
A parade of giggles, loud and bright,
Flickering banners bring pure delight.

As we march with quirky flair,
Pies fly by! Oh, beware! Beware!
Laughing when custard hits a hat,
Chasing joy, we bounce like a cat.

Lights are twinkling, oh so grand,
Funny faces, a clowning band.
With every twist, a pie takes flight,
In this whimsical world, all feels right.

Underneath the starry sky,
We burst with laughter, oh my, oh my!
Flickering dreams just out of sight,
In the moonglow, we dance tonight.

Cascades of Velvet Dreams

Rolling down the hill in style,
In capes and shades, we travel a mile.
Velvet whispers on the grass,
As we tumble, slip, and laugh en masse.

Bouncy castles sway and gleam,
While teensy fairies plot and scheme.
Spinning stories dressed in jest,
In cascades of dreams, we find our fest.

A balloon dog leads the way,
Chasing rain clouds that duck and sway.
With each brave leap and silly cheer,
We float on giggles, never fear.

Swinging high, we aim for the stars,
Echoes of laughter, no need for cars.
In this playful realm of make believe,
The velvet dreams we love, we weave.

Tattered Elegance in Motion

Dressed in stripes and polka dots,
With mismatched shoes, we show our spots.
A waltz of chaos, quite the scene,
In our tattered grace, we feel like queens.

As the music plays, we lose control,
Spinning wildly, we play our role.
Tripping over thoughts, we laugh and fall,
In this grand ballet, we do it all.

A touch of class wrapped in a flip,
With every misstep, we take a trip.
In charming blunders, we find our peace,
As elegance wobbles, our joy won't cease.

With every twirl, the world's our stage,
Simple antics free of rage.
Embracing flaws in this lovey-dove,
In tattered elegance, we rise above.

The Flicker of Wandering Strands

In the wind they dance and twirl,
Like a cat in a whirl,
Each twist brings giggles bright,
A sight that brings delight.

Flapping like a butterfly,
Trying to reach the sky,
With every gust they sway,
In a silly, frolicsome way.

They catch the eye and tease,
What a sight! Oh, look at these!
A game of chase, a playful sprout,
Wandering strands that twist about.

Oh, what a jolly jig they weave,
A tapestry that makes us believe,
In the joy of simple play,
In the breeze, they laugh away.

Cascades of Color in Motion

A splash of hues, bold and bright,
In the breeze, what a funny sight!
Each combo wiggles, laughs, and shimmies,
Like a party of giggling jimmies.

Swings and sways on a sunny day,
A rainbow's grin in a playful ballet,
With every turn, they twist and shout,
Dashed with whimsy, there's no doubt!

Chasing laughter in the air,
Colorful whispers everywhere,
A festival of shades that tease,
Swaying in tune with the gentle breeze.

They play like children, wild and free,
In a dance that's sheer jubilee,
With every flutter, a chuckle floats,
A cascade of joy, on breeze it coats.

Echoes of Playful Fibers

Silly strands just love to play,
In the wind, they prance all day,
Like whispers of jest, they parade,
In mirrors of laughter softly laid.

Each flutter sings a song of cheer,
Echoes of funny, loud and clear,
Wrapped in sunshine, twirls abound,
Giggling echoes all around.

They bounce and kick, a lively crowd,
In every gust, they're feeling proud,
Threads of jokes in a fabric maze,
Frolicking fibers leave us in a daze.

A tapestry of chuckles spun,
Where every loop is hefty fun,
In the wind, the humor flies,
A merry dance beneath the skies.

The Embrace of Woven Whispers

In the breeze, a playful hum,
Woven whispers, oh so fun!
Each flutter brings a joke or two,
Giggles wrapped in every hue.

They snicker softly, twirling round,
A hilarious game that can be found,
As they tumble and tease the air,
A silent laughter everywhere.

Knots and loops in bold embrace,
Woven tales of a friendly race,
Twigs and threads make quite a scene,
A joyous fabric, bright and keen.

Whispers float with whimsy's kiss,
In a dance you cannot miss,
Each turn a chuckle, a light-hearted spree,
A party of whimsy swaying free.

Gentle Aria of Sunlit Threads

A ribbon danced upon the air,
With every twist, it had a flair,
It twirled and spun, what a sight,
As if it joked with morning light.

The neighbors stopped to take a peek,
They wondered what the threads could speak,
A secret party, they assumed,
Of yarns and stories, brightly bloomed.

A gust of wind gave it a shove,
“Hey, stop that dance!” it seemed to love,
It winked with glee, and off it went,
A playful spirit, not content.

With swirling colors, laughter soared,
As threads of joy, the sun adored,
A puppet show of fabric dreams,
In every twitch, it softly beams.

The Caress of Whispered Fibers

The fibers wiggled with delight,
As sunlight peeked, a teasing light,
They shimmied, sparkled, bold and brash,
In the breeze, a vibrant splash.

Little birds would chirp and sway,
"Join us, come frolic, let's play!"
The threads would giggle, twist, and glide,
Like partygoers, full of pride.

A playful breeze just couldn't stop,
It tossed the strands, they spun and hop,
"The wind is wild!" the fibers cried,
So off they went, a tangled ride.

As shadows danced beneath the trees,
The laughter rose like whispers of ease,
With every flutter, every cheer,
The fibers knew they had no fear.

Playful Shadows of Culture

In gatherings where colors meet,
The playful threads could not be beat,
They pranced and preened, a lively crew,
A fabric fiesta, bright and true.

Each twist a tale of silly blends,
Of cultures rich, where laughter bends,
The fibers giggle, jump, and sway,
With woven jokes in every display.

“Come on,” they teased, “let’s frolic fast!”
A playful scene, shadows cast,
In every knot, a quirky laugh,
A dance of history, stitched by craft.

The sun became a spotlight bright,
A fabric show, a sheer delight,
With every thread, a vibrant cheer,
A tapestry of fun, sincere.

Tails that Tell Tales

With highlights bright, the strands would prance,
In pairs they'd twirl, a silly dance,
Each thread a tail with tales to weave,
In breezy whispers, hard to believe.

“Did you hear?” one thread would tease,
Of breezy antics, sweet as breeze,
“I misheard gossip from the sky,
Of clouds that laugh and rain that sigh.”

Twist it this way, flip it that,
The threads exchanged their chitchat chat,
Knots and tangles made a crew,
Spinning stories, fresh and new.

The sun began to dip and dive,
But threads stayed bright, they felt alive,
In every flutter, stories swell,
Those playful tails had much to tell.

The Play of Silken Appendages

In the garden, strings are dancing,
Flapping here and there, they're prancing.
A squirrel stops, gives a wink,
Wondering what they think!

Watch the ribbons twist and twine,
As if they've all had too much wine.
A breeze whispers secrets, a soft tease,
While petals blush, brought to their knees!

With every gust, they pirouette,
Creating chaos, no regret.
Chasing shadows, the sun beams bright,
What a sight, oh what a sight!

Like clowns in a circus, they jive and swirl,
Little giggles in nature unfurl.
A playful tease with each thumping beat,
Ribbons know how to make life sweet!

Lullabies in the Air

The trees hum softly, a melody so sweet,
While tiny flags dance a rhythmic beat.
A breeze that tickles the back of your neck,
Wakes up the snoozers with a gentle peck.

With a chuckle here and a flutter there,
They shimmy and shake, without a care.
Bumblebees join in with their buzz and bop,
Nature's laughter, a non-stop hop!

Oh look, a leaf joins the parade,
Spinning around in a leafy charade.
Swapping tales with a wandering cloud,
Even the sun seems to giggle out loud!

Who knew the world could wiggle and sway?
Even grumpy old oaks seem to play.
Together they laugh, sway, and jest,
In this caper, they've all been blessed!

Threads of Nature's Breath

A thread reached out for a game of tag,
With daisies nodding, they dance and brag.
Around the fence, they zoom and weave,
Caught in a whirl, they just won't leave!

The comic winds blow hot and cold,
Their antics unfolding, brave and bold.
A playful tangle, in giggles ensue,
Disguised as a mess, yet a grand debut!

With each soft blow, they prance anew,
In playful huddles, the breeze breaks through.
A jester's laughter fills the air,
Each jest of nature, a merry affair!

Who knew threads could have such flair?
As slim lines leap without a care.
In wind’s embrace, they’ve taken flight,
A dance of mirth, what a delight!

Swaying Chords of a Gentle Touch

Strums of laughter from the wilting grass,
Caterpillars groove, as the breezes pass.
A wiggly worm swings with flair,
Making all the other critters stare!

Gossamer whispers loom overhead,
Tickling leaves gently, as life's thread.
Nature’s tune plays like a happy song,
With flutters and flaps, we all belong!

The chorus of giggles, tumbling by,
As colors swirl in the azure sky.
Sunlight blinks, a cheeky spark,
With shadows dancing, a merry lark!

In the symphony of all things bright,
The world hums laughter, pure delight.
So sway with joy, and let it flow,
In a dance of whimsy that’s sure to glow!

The Journey of Waving Strands

In the park where whispers play,
Strings of joy join the fray.
They twirl and spin in the air,
Giving wind an odd scare.

A twist, a turn, then they slide,
Sneaking behind a cheeky ride.
With kites and kids in pure glee,
A merry dance for all to see.

Blowing kisses to passing cars,
Tickling noses beneath the stars.
Their giggles echo, laughter's song,
What a sight! Nothing feels wrong.

Though tangled in branches high,
They wiggle free, oh what a try!
With every leap, a happy cheer,
Life’s a dance, let’s hold it dear.

Buoyant Dances of Fabric

Bright colors flash, a yarn parade,
Frolicking lightly, never afraid.
They jiggle, they bounce, always in sync,
Doing the cha-cha, oh, don't you think?

A breeze arrives, an unexpected guest,
These knotted friends never let rest.
They tango with trees, play tag with the sky,
Each little tug makes them want to fly.

Caught on fingers, they flail about,
Silly antics that provoke a shout.
The sun shines bright, and so do they,
Waving hello throughout the day.

A sudden gust; they squeal with delight,
Chasing shadows into the night.
These ribbons of fun, a whimsical chase,
Wrapped in laughter, time can't erase.

Tailwinds of Fringed Creation

Fringes flutter with every gust,
Making friends with clouds, they trust.
They dance high, they dip low,
In playful rhythms, off they go.

Curly queues and wavy trails,
Hitching laughs to happy tales.
Every twist, a burst of mirth,
Celebrating this colorful birth.

They tumble, they swirl with flair,
Who knew wind could have such hair?
In a fabric world, absurd and bright,
It's a riot, a comical sight!

Snagged in doors with a gentle tug,
They bounce back with a playful shrug.
Oh, to be free, in wild ballet,
With one last spin, they sweep away.

Ribbons of Fleeting Thoughts

Thoughts like ribbons, drift and weave,
In the breeze, they dance and leave.
One whispers, "Catch me if you can!"
Another giggles, "I'm just a plan!"

In the park, under playful skies,
They share their dreams with sparkling eyes.
As the wind plays its mischievous game,
Each strand of mind feels wild and tame.

A flurry of ideas, here and there,
Chasing with laughter, beyond compare.
They spin in circles, tickling the day,
Crafting stories in a breezy display.

From sunny rays to a sudden storm,
These thoughts fly by, never conform.
But oh what joy, in the fleeting race,
Life's a tapestry, a joyous chaos.

www.ingramcontent.com/pod-product-compliance
Lightning Source LLC
Chambersburg PA
CBHW060126230426
43661CB00003B/346
* 9 7 8 1 8 0 5 8 6 1 2 6 3 *